ropewalk
angela carr

ropewalk

angela carr

SNARE BOOKS . MONTREAL . 2006

Edited by Robert Allen
Designed by Jon Paul Fiorentino
Typeset in Goudy Old Style

Library and Archives Canada Cataloguing in Publication

Carr, Angela, 1976-
    Ropewalk : poems / Angela Carr.

ISBN-13: 978-0-9739438-2-5
ISBN-10: 0-9739438-2-3

    I. Title.

PS8605.A773R66 2006   C811'.6   C2006-904941-6

Printed and bound in Canada

Represented in Canada by the Literary Press Group
Agented by Conundrum Press

SNARE BOOKS
#1A - 4302 St. Urbain Street
Montreal QC
H2W 1V5
snarebooks.wordpress.com

I'd have liked us to talk a while longer
but of words too at the peak of their perfection
their fall from the midst of mirrors

Nicole Brossard

contents

ropewalk

The Louise Labé Poems

Ropewalk: A long, covered walk or a low-level building where ropes are manufactured.

In long and narrow alleyways yarns are stretched out between revolving hooks 300 yards apart. These yarns are wound into ropes suitably long for use on tall ships. This method of rope-making, the rope-walk, was in use during the Renaissance; ropes were made from flax or hemp; the part of the plant used was the bast; the strength of the rope was measured in grams/denier (an old silk measure).

Of bow strings none remain.

Whenever I braid my hair, the mistaking of one smaller strand makes for an unbalanced plait, one that is impossible to complete, for the thinner strand slips from my finger, unwinding. It is easier to achieve two strands of equal strength; balance is given more easily to two than three; strolling groups diverge into couples; the Easter sun races through dusk, night and day forming the largest portion. So the braid undoes itself.

This

This is the case with Louise Labé, myself, and the much conjectured third party who was the object of her sonnets, her lover. One of us is too thin; most often it is myself or the beloved (whom I have called H). One of us is too thin, the braid unwinds, the hair is wild, words flying left and right with no rational temper. I know too little about myself, and even less about the beloved, the ghost of a ghost.

The beloved I call

The beloved I call H after Henri, the French dauphin and then king in Louise's lifetime. According to myth, Louise single-handedly defeated an entire army at Perpignan when accompanying this future king to war. A second story places her, in the same year, participating in a fencing tournament for the dauphin during a carnival to celebrate his appearance in Lyons. Whether she fought, really, or figuratively, in the year 1542, with a sword in one hand, is a question. In this capacity, the swordswoman, she is known as le Capitaine Loys. That she loved Henri is a rumour.

capitaine loys facts infrequent
lettered and under testimony
roamed carnivals in drag
a secret merchant class fact: who
was class? fact? women
wearing letters on their chest
formed acrostics for the dauphin
but we are concerned with god's
not tentative testimony are we

The beloved I call H after history, for it is an historical act to give a name.

Many say that Olivier de Magny fell in love with Louise in 1554; her Oeuvres was published in 1555. Olivier was a fellow poet and a regular of her salon, the literary centre of Lyons, where he attended her with rapture, enamoured. A poem he published in 1559, Ode a Sire Aymon, ridicules a rope-maker: undoubtedly Ennemond, Louise's husband. There are two sorts of ties: the first is made with rope, and the second with the silvery lute string. A rope is coarse, clumsy, common, heavy; a lute string is delicate, refined, lustrous, quivering.

when my eyes, as my lute
have rent that tender cord
tears: a broken string

A sonnet is published by Louise Labé and another by Olivier de Magny; they are, excepting spelling variations, exactly the same up to the final sestet.

Later, in immense new lands surprisingly athwart
Olivier de Magny: his prolonged absence provokes
Under and navigating by stars
an Increasing number of poems
a Soft chair in the salon stands empty
Elsewhere, new land a utensil, he eats

These last hours of her maidenhood
she becomes available. What's valence
and what's opposite : in the centre a trunk,
on the outskirts, leaves

I'd like to see her draw her sword
and slice
through the page in which she's pictured.
Then
I could catch her bouquet.

Lettered and under testimony
Of trees
U
In which she's pictured
She becomes available

H	E	N	R	I
e			u	n
r			m	
			o	t
v			u	h
e			r	e
i			e	s
l			d	e
i				l
s				e
				a
				v
				e
				s

Come death, of my envies ease

Is each eye a ring then? What
is the girth of the sun? Cares
my thirst for shops?

                              If the
beloved said to me, Dear friend,
vie for the tree, would I be for the tree?
What if these arms were torn from me?

Literature and the sciences are accustomed to bear this
acOllé arms holding it
    Under customs of cut and paste
    In as much as faces iceux my touching heart
 a Spark was stolen from you
    Even so, erroneous

Does the line last longer
than the point at which you wanted me?
After a time.
Am I fragile at this point you wanting me?
Am I lasting at this point?
Am I coming at this point and is it lasting?
Am I nettles?
Are you burning in this point?
Am I centered in your beauty and is it cold and are we holding?

Orbital dwelling, a valence
lover far from the heart:
a swimmer with a toe in.

I am this tenant. My life
arrows toward :

Lovers ghost.

venoit death, my envious ease
the lovers' are blind eyes, i have them already

In *Notes sur la fortune posthume de Louise Labé*, Enzo Guidici collects twenty-seven short pieces of fiction inspired by the lack of biography for Labé. She was a favourite of the romantics, one of whom altered her sole existing portrait for a softer and prettier lady.

Leaving no evidence
Of her stay
Unsimilar tongue
Into soft running to avoid it-
Self
Turn Eye, turn

Where are Love's dangerous arrows
        O so many goods
      VagUely sweet as though
         I could not say who came by boat and who
         S
         Estimate or mirror

Left with little evidence
Of you this is known
Upwardly mobile artisan class
Including both text and criticism
Sonnets and
Ease guesses also

Sun towards me turn
Eyes, turn contraries

Cordelier: 1) A Franciscan Friar of the strict rule, so called because of the knotted cord worn around the waist. 2) Name of one of the political clubs of the French revolution (club des cordeliers) so called because it met in an old convent of the cordeliers. 3) Name given to a machine for rope-making.

To think water, that is all and alL

        Overwhelming any map
        Unreported, unremembered
   wrIst controlled, under
        Shades of service
        Evaporates

to Love morning
       Of love a constant source
       Unecessarily love
   wind In the city this love
within its wallS
       Endless loop

cite love never a continuous layer
only a city within morning
without thinking I treuve it out of sorrow
in this strata
source misfortune
entremeslez joy

imprimeurs de Roy

	ung oat ill ion
Lyons as an important	ung aultre ilion
	un gaull trellion
	un gaule tre lyon
red leaves in ink	in gaul **letre** lyon
	in gul **let** rely on
	in gu**let** rall ion
	ing **let** rally un
	ing **letral** ly ung

small burning absences
ever as good as

looped hybrid

flesches   arrested

                                earlier

technological image   contiguous with towers

hit.

easier illusion   city tree

newly appropriated   I

                        was dreaming   how of all

words

 throw   my arrows
in vain

empty cups

Empty Cups

For the first year there was a party. Take red weddings and bland weddings because a man rents an elk. His two eyes appear black stars see the elks shine them palpate them re-light them. The air is a species a ghost.

no plates

he just walked in
off the ice they
towed his car
with no plates
what
to do

my meal
unfinished confused
with food

there was a man
who lived with grizzlies
and was eventually
eaten by one he said
all of the hype
around bears you've
got to accept

even babies can
die de deux
choses l'une l'autre i
never talk about
the saddest

surface of
so it's brilliant
apocalyptic cold
blowing in

Spine

This spine with baptizer. A name in abeyance. Atop the slide I open the here. The here are opening. The here are your tiny or many spines. Your dyed-blue hair trembling down the here are many openings.

self portrait

for xenia

she is before a door.
before a door, she is adored.

for her, not the door, but what is behind a door,
for she is not before a door, but
is adored.

for her, what is behind the door,
for she is not before a door, but
before a doorway and there
there are many dancing.

but she more frequently
is not dancing. she is before
a hall and there
there are many dancing.

she crouches,
not watching dancing, not dancing.
before a door that is not a doorway
for her frequently

Kicking

This kicking one changes her world. Elects representatives and middle muscles. Unmakes dangerous lakes. Unwonders colours. How easily a map is crumpled. Leaving no evidence of her stay, no scent soaked into the hardbearing muscle or marrow. Stretch mark here

Below the ninth month

Here we are, seated on the warehouse roof on Neufmont again. Heavy, sweet snows ambulate forms from the sleeping skies. Months are solid, dense things and the living warm their hands over a fire. When, below the ninth month, my cervix ripens, I will seek out your face from a crowd and in the process I will drop this paper. Because I will vanish into this, odourous, ugly, moaning.

in an envelope

I have it in an envelope
sealed I tasted the glue before
kicking myself because
of course I do not want to send it.
What use is it anyhow to catalogue
my and the kids' fevers.
I might as well be writing
with a French keyboard, fucking
up all the symbols. The stamp
on the envelope is one of these
windows you can't even see through.
Sometimes a disk ejects spontaneously
and now there are blisters all over their mouths
and they hurt. I said Drink some water

translating josé marti

I slow the horseman

his
careful
serious
seat
visible

at
eye
level
just beside my head

typing
long hours
into the
formal
air

so that
I may enter
nude

giant slats

        on   suitably   giant   windows

the sound of the escalator   minnows

smallest green ions

                under water

i like this space   feet folding under   under

      farther and farther from the beauty quotient

silent angle   even the silencing carpet   library

        moons   neonmetroarrow   above

and below the glassline   under the surface

carlightslide   satellite

a sieve receives   separates the raincoat from the clothing

the raincoat from its colour

the raincoat from   green light   impermeable

chlor

thirst   an impossibly unstained new

page   BIENVENUE like

naked   longing

licking windows   glass as high as any dream

thirst

distraction traffic shelves   lamps legal
          getting legal water walking here

security mobile or stationary   crotch

                    to thirst is   luminous

security on the move might suspect   even these fingers
that touch

a woman unraveling her beauty

touching metal is like   putting glasses on

                                                                     yes
                                                                     metal generally

putting glasses on is like   saying no thank you

glass and metal   cold winter surface

contact inevitable I

world frozen on the glass

contact   inevitable   denied

                is like   denied

the following page, her absence

i.

twelve ants suspended in honey
small corner movement an ear
from the north to santiago
summer behind blinds

ii.

question mark of her hand at the end of the beautiful
odour of the second page torn out
rain falling once there were rails there
to be scarred by no space

iii.

the space between eyes and hands widens
confining the world to a style
lying beside the mississippi i can have
hips ankles feet dandelions

iv.

ants cooling down the walls
panic within the rain
on either side of a bed silver empty
no equivalence no reality

mountance of a dream

Mountance of a Dream

The mountance of a dream is the length of time required to travel a dream.
I elect the house, and the threats to the house.

A mouse travels the kitchen walls, clinging like an insect, but of course larger, and furry. The wood beams are unfinished; they are also furry. This is a poor person's house, the mice scurry over their mother's body. I awaken the cat. Having trapped a mouse effortlessly, she prepares to eat. When the squeaking ceases, I reflect on how those utterances were like sounds my daughter and I made, pretending to be mice, although neither of us had ever heard one.

In the second dream I am in the house and someone is trying to get in. They are in the front and then the back in an instant. A cat is slipped through the mail slot, a thin cat we catch effortlessly.

Three branches hover in the breeze at the window.

The next night

It is so dark I cannot see the branches; the window instead offers reflections. I am in the country, driving down a two-wheel tractor road in a small truck. The woman with me has brought three objects; one for each of the two brothers who are in love with her; the third is a child's stuffed mouse. When at the house their father speaks, it becomes apparent that the first two objects are those that the brothers have chosen; for this reason I cannot recall what they are, not having been chosen by her.

The animal spirits responsible for memory are neither animal nor spirit. Memory is a mainspring for discomfort. Wriggling figures are dissected on the first tables of the Royal Society. Eels, worms, wet fish: the way memory feels, a wet slippery thing at the foot of the bed.

(No longer the woman who writes, she is the house in which the family is turned to stone. This half-hearted conversation on the landing is infinite. Stairs,
coated in a translucent

animal spirit

Maybe any name is a house.

I climb up the stairs and on the landing stop
To look at a collage: photographs, gold paper, at waist
Height as if hung by a child. In each
Sky bisecting the landscape. A butterfly.
There is my face in the mirror the child holds
Up to her face, what a strange effect, stray

Maybe this, my face

I climb the stairs and then a second set of stairs
Lines, inverted stairs: scores in the deep bark
Elm and crescent owl, ginger-coloured eyes like mine
Clawing at a branch each metal string
Reverberates, like the remembered image.
That is my home, in the hands of a woman
Who resembles everything of the past.

some nights there are no dreams

it is cold i sit
hovering
ghostlike not
quite alive

drink water try
to clear the rub-
ble from my
throat

Learn fear.
Discovered in the dark as alive.

She is bearing it up the metro stairs.
She polishes its shiny skin
while hiding it under her coat.

Fear, as though wet.
These grown-up fingers
can't hide anything.

If the tongue were a leaf I would be silent all winter.

If time was singular and without grief, time was.

      (should be married instead and i remember the twilight of this
arrangement spring on the deck and the light the colour of pine
      needles)

There is my hand in water

There is water but fear is colder
Harder in the throat like words

God's many atrocities fossilized

Labé was to Calvin *a common whore*

When the phone rings don't answer it
   Or do this time it's
   Someone I haven't spoken to in so long
   Intentionally avoided
   Kept myself my daughter from

   Sadness could be caused by

I climb the stairs and enter a child's playground.
A man swings on the bars, nostrils full of sand,
And shouts

                                                    A wall
I could feel with my hand dissolves when I try
To lean on it. Inside myself
I feel nothing.

I climb the stairs at the open door
Remove my shoes
Wet socks then too.
Each step is a leaf. The leaves
Are thick glass cut
To look like glass.

If at the top of the stairs I shed myself effortlessly

The rain is falling

The rain is bearing news
More efficiently than TV.

Hisses

If at the top of the stairs I shed my self effortlessly

Werewolves tonight I fill the pool
With carrot juice and something rose
Only an inch deep so far and the rest
Of them off to the movies

Too diluted: its potency
Is doubtful. How to affect death
To the werewolf?

So where shall I hide
From the wereworld. Under the
Bed in the corridor the bed at the
Window the cold and crystal window under
The bedframe between the springs and the mattress
Between mattresses like a penny

In the deeper past my standard self, a roll of coins
My metallic equivalent
I drank from flasks then the Calvinist water
From any spring

one row of red curtains the third floor of the school
the middle floor the line of symmetry the centered horizon
red and weightless

namely mother with the deep line down
the centre of her belly
ascribed us to ideas and them to us of course

       silence in the coat room with a migraine
       and in the room with the high mahogany bedframe
       mossing underneath it
       near the springs

I climb the stairs   I climb   over easily
green hills   and   easy   No summit
to be reached   Here   a room then

a room   A soft white sofa and a man
talking on a cellular phone   Small
passport-type photos taped   to this phone

These are photos of him   the man talking

"The phone," he says, "is dirty   but we cannot find
the correct soap.   Have you seen the soap? We cannot find the soap."

"The phone," he says, "is blocked, clogged, is   furred up
with images."   and as I get closer I see

He is a photo a   life-sized photo   he is
a screen

Still.

A stopped watch. Soft time soft ache in the eyelids, shovels, the eyelids are a feverish green. The fever is a dark green vegetable, darker than spinach or rapini. There the little baby feet, pummeling the green. There guilt in dreams. The feet in the eyes, the silent: kicking over of a fever. Here. Read over kicked over darker than tea on the hem of the green overalls and the tears that resulted from contact with the tea. I do not mean to write with brevity or of mysteries.

To turn over, to wait for, a cash register, the turning of, the transition from then to now, from now to then, to recess. A pit in the earth. A throat.

My first memory is a set of stairs.

No escape, the set of stairs leading up to no floor.

The flanking timbrous walls
are thick; together
they make the stairway narrow.

I must move
straight and thin as an officer's whistle
to ascend.

Here, ascending from no-water to over

                                    no-water

It is not an escape.
There is no escape.
For those who feel the need to escape.

Acknowledgements

Thanks to the editors of *The Donkey Journal*, *Matrix*, and *Slingshot*. Thanks to Mary di Michele who read many of these poems in earlier versions, for her enduring support and tenderness. Thanks to Robert Allen and Jon Paul Fiorentino at Snare for their openness, brilliance and design. Thanks to Oana Avasilichioaei, visionary, for seeing and for refreshing. Thanks to Xenia Fedorchenko for artwork, for entangling the ropes. Thanks to Melissa Weinstein, poet and beekeeper, for generous writing and reading. Thanks to Brenda Cockfield for her friendship, skills and wit. Thanks to Tomas Diaz for his extraordinary patience. Por Isidora y Neve and the future.

No Escape, a sculpture by Louise Bourgeois.

"I'd have liked us to talk a while longer..." *Museum of Bone and Water*
by Nicole Brossard (transl. by Robert Majzels and Erin Mouré)

MEMBER OF SCABRINI GROUP

Québec, Canada
2006